j944 T484L
Thomson, Ruth, 1957-
Living in Fr___
WITHDRAWN
APR 1 6 2008

D0535688

Living in
France

Ruth Thomson
Photography by David Hampton

SEA-TO-SEA
Mankato Collingwood London

This edition first published in 2007 by
Sea-to-Sea Publications
1980 Lookout Drive
North Mankato
Minnesota 56003

Copyright © Sea-to-Sea Publications 2007

Printed in China

All rights reserved

Library of Congress Cataloging-in-Publication Data

Thomson, Ruth, 1949-
    Living in France / by Ruth Thomson.
      p. cm. -- (Living in--)
    Includes index.
    ISBN-13: 978-1-59771-042-8 7971606
  1. France--Juvenile literature. 2. France--Social life and customs--Juvenile
  literature. I. Title: France. II. Title. III. Series.

DC33.7.T56 2006
944--dc22
                                                                    2005058175

9 8 7 6 5 4 3 2

Published by arrangement with the Watts Publishing Group Ltd, London

Series editor: Ruth Thomson
Series designer: Edward Kinsey
Photographs by David Hampton except
 page 9 Wimenet, Parc du Futuroscope

With thanks to Virginia Chandler

Contents

This is France

France is the second-biggest country in Europe. The French call it "the Hexagon" because of its six-sided shape. It has borders with six other countries.

The island of Corsica in the Mediterranean and the distant lands of Guiana in South America, Guadeloupe and Martinique in the Caribbean, and Réunion in the Indian Ocean are part of the French nation too.

△ **Dense forests**
Forests cover one-quarter of the country. They give timber for industry, shelter for wildlife, and are popular with hikers.

△ **The coastline**
The sea borders three sides of France. The Atlantic coast of Brittany is wild and rugged. Its rocky inlets shelter busy fishing ports.

◁ **Lush pastures**
France has an ideal climate for farming. In the west, farms have orchards and small hedged fields where dairy cattle graze.

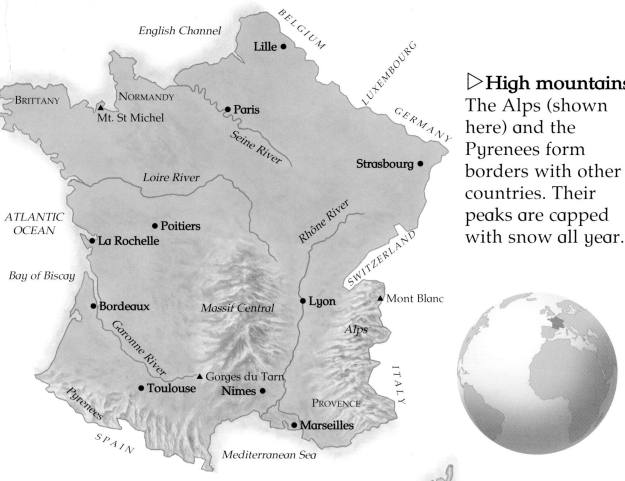

BELGIUM
LUXEMBOURG
GERMANY
SWITZERLAND
ITALY
SPAIN

English Channel
Lille •
NORMANDY
▲ Mt. St Michel
BRITTANY
• Paris
Seine River
Strasbourg •
Loire River
ATLANTIC OCEAN
• Poitiers
• La Rochelle
Rhône River
Bay of Biscay
• Bordeaux
Massif Central
• Lyon
▲ Mont Blanc
Garonne River
Alps
▲ Gorges du Tarn
• Toulouse
Nimes •
PROVENCE
• Marseilles
Mediterranean Sea
Pyrenees

CORSICA

▷ High mountains

The Alps (shown here) and the Pyrenees form borders with other countries. Their peaks are capped with snow all year.

◁ The sunny south

The hot, sunny Mediterranean coast is crowded in summer with millions of people on vacation. Olive and fruit trees, fields of lavender, and herbs grow inland.

Fact Box

Capital: Paris
Population: 58.6 million
Official language: French
Main religion: Roman Catholic
Highest mountain: Mont Blanc (15,770 ft/4,807 m)
Longest river: Loire (629 miles/1,012 km)
Biggest cities: Marseilles, Lyon, Lille, Toulouse, Bordeaux
Currency: Euro

Paris—the capital

Paris is by far the biggest and most important city in France. One in five French people live in the capital and its surrounding area. It is the center of French government and of banking and business, culture, and fashion. It is also the hub of the country's road and railroad network.

△**The Champs Elysées**
Military parades and the last stage of the Tour de France bicycle race take place on this wide avenue.

◁ **The Eiffel Tower**
More than 1,050 feet (320 m) high, this iron tower was built in 1889 for the Universal Exhibition. It took two years to build, using more than two million rivets!

▽ **La Défense**
Thousands of people work in a huge office building shaped like an arch in La Défense, one of the business centers of Paris.

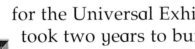

△**Notre Dame**
This Gothic cathedral stands on an island, the Ile de la Cité, in the middle of the Seine River

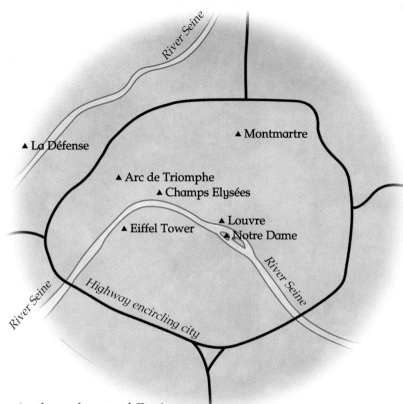

A plan of central Paris

The world capital of tourism

The museums and monuments of Paris are famous the world over. Eleven million foreign tourists flock to Paris each year to see its sights, to eat in its famous restaurants, and to shop in its exclusive stores.

△ **The Seine River**
The Seine River runs through Paris, crossed by 37 bridges. Visitors can take a ride along the river on a boat called a *bâteau mouche*.

▷ **The Louvre**
Once the palace of French kings, the Louvre is the world's biggest art museum. The entrance is under a modern glass pyramid.

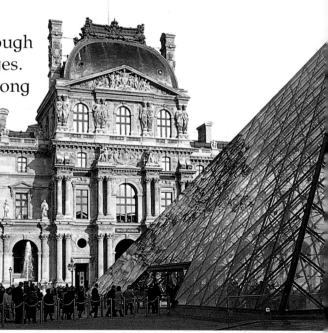

Famous sights

France is full of treasures from its long and rich history. Cave paintings of animals and hunters date back to prehistoric times. Traces of the Roman conquest, when the country was called Gaul, can be seen in ruined villas, amphitheaters, and bridges.

Every period has left its mark—from the cathedrals, towns, and castles of the Middle Ages and the castles (*châteaux*) of Renaissance nobles, to the most up-to-date buildings of today.

△ **The Maison Carrée, Nîmes**
The Romans built a city, with temples, theaters, and public baths, in Nîmes, in the south of France. This Roman temple honored the grandsons of the emperor Augustus.

▷ **Mont Saint Michel**
This monastery was built on top of a granite island off the Normandy coast, in the Middle Ages. Now it has a million visitors a year.

8

△ The Tarn Gorge

France is also famous for its natural wonders. The rushing Tarn River in southern France has cut spectacular gorges through the rocks.

A selection of tourist guides and brochures

△ The Château of Chambord

Chambord is the largest of the châteaux in the Loire valley. King François I transformed the medieval castle into a splendid Renaissance palace with 440 rooms and 83 staircases.

△ Futuroscope

The Futuroscope theme park, near Poitiers, houses the latest audio-visual shows. Its futuristic buildings include movie theaters with circular or 3-D screens.

9

Living in towns and cities

More than three-quarters of French people live in cities or towns. Many town centers are full of historic buildings, which have often been cleaned and restored.

The heart of a city is usually a large square (*place*) where the town hall stands. Above its door flies the French flag, the *Tricolore* (three colors). The *place* may have restaurants and cafés, with a church and market nearby.

△**Riverside towns**
Most towns are situated on or near one of France's many rivers. Sometimes, violent rains can cause damaging floods.

◁**The mayor**
Every city, town, and village elects a council, with a mayor as its leader. The mayor wears the *Tricolore* sash of office for ceremonies.

△**Car-free streets**
Cars are banned from many city center streets and squares. These are pleasant, safe places to stroll and go shopping.

◁ **Town church**
All towns have a large church or cathedral near the center. The main religion in France is Roman Catholicism. However, fewer people go to church regularly now than in the past.

▽ **Town signs**
On the road into every town or village is a sign with its name. On the way out of town is the same sign with a line through it. This sign shows the road number as well.

△ **Apartments**
Many people live on the outskirts of large towns, in apartment buildings.

Most areas have local tourist brochures

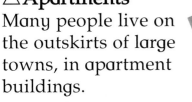

D 110
LA JARRIE

Around town

Cafés are a central part of town life. They open from early morning till late at night for coffee, drinks, and food. People of all ages come to meet their friends, read the newspapers provided, play cards, or the pinball machine (*le flipper*), or watch a soccer game on the bar TV.

△ **City faces**
Over the years, people of many countries and races have come to live and work in France. Many have French nationality.

◁ **Children's menu**
Some restaurants serve inexpensive three-course meals for children.

▷ **Street cafés**
People enjoy sitting outside at cafés to watch the world go by. The tables are shaded by awnings.

▽A Morris column

This pillar-shaped billboard advertises the latest movies, concerts, or plays.

Evenings in town

Town centers are often lively in the evening. The cafés fill up again, as people leave work and meet for a drink before going to a restaurant, the movies, or the theatre.

◁Parks

Town parks are very well looked after. They have gravel paths and formal flowerbeds.

◁Opening times

In smaller towns, stores shut for two hours or more at lunchtime. But they stay open in the evening.

△Street signs

French streets—and schools and public buildings—are often named after a saint or a famous person. Voltaire was a French writer of the 18th century.

13

Living in the country

Farming has always been important to France. Farmland covers more than half the country. It produces enough food both to feed its people and to sell abroad.

Sixty years ago, half of the population lived in the country. Today, it's only one-quarter. In rich farming areas, modern machines and methods can produce more food than before, with fewer workers.

▷ **Vineyards**
Wine is one of France's most valuable products. Vineyards are found in most regions. Growers prune the vines by hand.

◁ **A country treasure**
In the fall, country people hunt for prized wild mushrooms. They may sell these at the local village market.

△ **The village square**
Most villages have a square with a church and a memorial to local people killed in the two World Wa

▽Country homes
Once, country farms and houses were built in the local style, using the stone, brick, or wood of the region. New homes tend to all look alike and are built of the same modern materials.

△Modern farming
On the fertile plains, farmers use enormous, expensive machines to spray and harvest crops in vast, open fields.

Empty villages
Young people are leaving the country to find work in towns. As villages in remote areas empty, their stores and schools close. Villages near big cities thrive because commuters move into new houses built on farmland.

◁Traveling store
As village stores close down, country people depend on visits from the traveling grocer, butcher, and baker in their vans.

Shopping

Busy modern life means people find it easier to go shopping in out-of-town "hypermarkets." These giant stores sell everything under one roof—food, TVs, furniture, computers, and home-renovation supplies. They open for long hours and are cheap.

The French appreciate fresh, high-quality food and still use specialist stores. They enjoy going to the local market, which is a social event as well as a chance to buy local produce.

Butcher (*Boucherie*)

Fishmonger (*Poissonerie*)

Supermarket sign

△**Pastry bakery (*pâtisserie*)**
Pâtisseries sell fruit tarts, éclairs, meringues, and other pastries. Fancy cakes can be made to order for a special occasion.

▷**French bread**
The baker (*boulangerie*) is open every day of the year! The traditional *baguette* (seen here) goes stale quickly, so people buy it fresh once, or often twice, each day.

▷**Local stores**
Specialist food stores offer high-quality produce. Supermarkets often sell clothes and items for the home as well as food.

◁ A retail park
Superstores are grouped around a vast parking lots on the outskirts of cities. It is hard for small stores in town to compete with them.

▷ Tobacconist (*tabac*)
Places that sell tobacco always have an orange "carrot" sign on the outside. They sell lottery tickets, phone cards, postage stamps, greeting cards, candy, and cigarettes.

◁ The market
Every town has a market at least once a week, selling fruit, vegetables, and cheese. Some stands sell local produce, such as eggs or herbs.

The tabac *sells a wide range of items.*

On the move

The French are fond of cars. Eight out of ten families own a car. They mostly buy French models—Renault, Peugeot, or Citroën. People prefer to drive to work, and to use their cars for weekend trips and vacations.

More than 3,728 miles (6,000 km) of highways link towns in France. These have frequent parking places (*aires*) where motorists can rest and eat.

△ Cycling
In towns, bicycle lanes are often separated from other road traffic, to make cycling safe.

▷ A moped (*mobylette*)
Mopeds and scooters are popular with young people. They can ride these from the age of 14, after passing a test.

▷ Highway tolls
Drivers take a ticket just before they join a highway (*autoroute*). When they leave it, they pay a toll, according to the distance they have traveled.

Toll receipt

Highway sign

3 A 16

200 m

◁**The Normandy Bridge**

This great bridge, more than one mile long, spans the Seine River in Normandy. It links northern and western France.

△**Michelin man**

Bibendum is the mascot of Michelin tires. He appears on Michelin maps, guides, and advertisements.

◁**High-speed trains**

The TGV travels at 125 miles (200 km) an hour. It takes 3 hours to travel from Paris to Marseilles.

◁**Punching tickets**

Passengers must punch their tickets in a machine before boarding their train.

▽**The métro**

However long the journey on a *métro*, the ticket always costs the same. People can save money by buying ten tickets at a time.

Trains

The railroad system is very efficient. High-speed trains, known as TGV (*Train à Grande Vitesse*), zoom between cities. Slower trains go to the suburbs and between towns. Big cities, such as Paris, Lyon, and Marseilles, have a subway system, called the *métro*.

Family life

The French think family life is important. Different generations may live farther away from one another than in the past, but they often get together for holidays and reunions. In the school vacation, grandparents may look after children of working parents.

Most homes have all the latest equipment. Nearly all of them have a TV, and half own two. There are terrestrial channels, plus pay TV, cable, and satellite.

△ **Evening meals**
Three out of four French women go out to work. But most families still eat together in the evening, at around 8 p.m.

△ **Family pets**
France holds the European record for the number of pets. One in three families has a dog, one in five a cat.

◁ **Sunday lunch**
Weekends often mean a big family meal at grandma's home in the country, or at a restaurant.

▷ **Weekend outings**
Weekends are a chance to enjoy the outdoors together—hiking, cycling, or going to a soccer, rugby, or basketball game.

△Games

Video and computer
games are popular and
so are comic books.

△Happy birthday! (*Joyeux Anniversaire!*)

The French celebrate birthdays with a
cake and cards. They often
sing the happy birthday
song in English!

*Asterix and Lucky Luke are
among the favorite comic-
book characters for both
children and adults.*

Time to eat

France is well known for its fine cooking and its good restaurants. The French always mark a special occasion with a grand meal, with five courses or more.

France produces a huge variety of foods. Every region is known for its own particular local produce or dish.

△**Seafood**
Platters of freshly caught oysters, mussels, crab, and other shellfish are served in restaurants by the sea.

△**Foreign flavors**
Immigrants have brought their own specialties. In big cities, there may be Algerian, Tunisian, Vietnamese, and Chinese grocery stores and restaurants.

Cassoulet from southwestern France—a dish of beans, sausages, and duck

Dijon mustard

Olives from the south of France

Three of the 400 French cheeses

Mineral water from Evian

Lentils from central France

Boar pâté from central France

Sweet pancake from Brittany

Sardines from Brittany

Dried sausage from the Auvergne

Oil and herbs from Provence

22

▷ Breakfast

A typical breakfast is cereal or a slice of crusty bread and jam, fruit juice, yogurt, and a bowl of hot chocolate.

◁ All sorts of bread

As well as bread, bakers sell sweet breads, buttery croissants, chocolate-filled croissants, and raisin buns, which people often buy for breakfast.

△ Eating out

In summer, squares and sidewalks are crowded with restaurant tables. People may spend several hours enjoying their meal.

◁ Fast food

Many traditional restaurants have given way to fast-food outlets. These sell burgers, sandwiches, pancakes, and pizzas.

23

School time

In France, children must go to school from 6 to 16 years of age. Most start at the age of three, in a state nursery school, and stay at school until they are 18. French children have the longest school day in Europe.

Primary school is from 9 a.m. till 5 p.m. (with a two-hour break for a three-course lunch, often in the canteen). There is homework to do after school. Much of the day is spent on reading, spelling, grammar and math—and there is no religious education.

◁ **Free time**
There is no school on Wednesday afternoons. That is the time for playing sports in local clubs, or other activities, such as music or dancing.

△ **One-class school**
Unlike most schools, this country school has only one class and one teacher. Children of varying ages are grouped together. For secondary school, they will journey by bus to the nearest town.

▷ School equipment

Children have to buy their own exercise books, pens, and ruler. The white board is for quick spelling tests in class.

△ Saturday school

In some towns, there is school on Saturday mornings instead of Wednesday mornings.

▷ School books

Pupils keep their books at home, and take what they need to school each day. Their school bags can be very heavy— some even have wheels!

Drawing book

Class workbook

Grammar exercise book

Music exercise book

Handwriting book

Pupil's school report

25

Having fun

With five weeks of vacation time a year and shorter working hours than in the past, the French have plenty of leisure time. Seven out of ten people play sports. They prefer individual ones such as tennis, skiing, or judo.

The major team sport is soccer—young players dream of joining the *Bleus*, the French national team, winners of the World Cup in 1998 and European champions in 2000.

△ **Pétanque**
The aim of this popular game is to bowl a heavy metal ball as close as possible to a small wooden one.

△ **Inline skating**
Some towns organize car-free Sundays, when inline skaters, cyclists, and walkers can take over the streets for the day.

◁ **Table soccer**
Coin-operated table soccer games are often found in cafés and youth clubs.

◁**Family picnic**
On fine weekends, people from towns and cities often spend the day in the countryside.

△**Multiplex movie theater**
Out-of-town multiscreen movie theaters show up to 15 different movies at a time. Young people may go several times a month.

Going on outings
Many French enjoy fishing, hunting, or having large family picnics. They also love going to the movies. Increasingly, they have DVD players for watching movies at home.

▷**Video kiosk**
People can rent a video, using a credit card, at any time of day or night at one of these automatic kiosks.

Vacations and celebrations

At the beginning of July and August, roads and railroad stations are packed as the French set off on vacation. The great majority of them stay in France.

Half go to the seaside, but nearly as many go to the countryside or mountains for activity holidays—hiking, kayaking, or climbing. Many save a week of their vacation for winter sports in the Alps or Pyrenees.

▽ Sightseeing
The French are proud of their heritage. They like to explore historical sites and monuments during their vacation.

△ Going to the seaside
Visitors crowd the beaches in summer. Some resorts organize beach clubs with games and activities for children.

◁ Vacation activities
Camping, waterskiing, walking, and fishing are popular vacation activities

◁ **Food festivals**
Many regions hold fairs to celebrate their local produce. At this apple fair, people can sample many different varieties, as well as buy tarts and jams, juice, and cider.

△ **A pardon**
In Brittany, saints' days are marked with a pardon, when villagers parade in their traditional costumes with music and dancing.

▷ **Bastille day, July 14**
This national holiday celebrates the attack on the Bastille prison at the start of the French Revolution in 1789. A funfair comes to town, people dance, and there are fireworks.

Fairs and festivals

Throughout France, festivities mark special occasions. Some are linked to religion, like the Carnival parades before Lent. Others celebrate country traditions or a particular season of the year. Some are related to local or national historical events.

Going further

Look for French food

Have a good look in a supermarket and see how many foods you can find that have come from France.

What sorts of foods are they? Do the labels tell you which part of France they come from? Find the places on a map of France. What types of food come from each region?

Find a French pen pal

Ask your relatives, teachers, friends, and neighbors if they know anyone of your age who lives in France and who might like to write to you. Tell your pen pal about your home, your interests, and your friends.

Trade some postcards, stamps, and stickers. Keep a scrapbook of things your pen pal sends you.

Make a tourist leaflet

Make a tourist leaflet about Paris or a French place that interests you.

Fold a piece of paper into three overlapping flaps. Glue down some pictures cut out from magazines, newspapers, or vacation brochures. Write short captions about them.

A useful place to get brochures and information about sights and places is: French Tourist Office,
444 Madison Avenue
New York, NY 10022

Telephone: (514) 288 1904

Websites

www.yahooligans.com/
Around_the_world/countries/France

www.sitesatlas.com/Europe/France

www.ambafrance-us.org/kids/

Glossary

Audio-visual The technology of sound and images used in movies and television.

Commuter A worker, living in the country or the town suburbs, who travels every day to work in a city business or office.

Currency The money used in a country.

French Revolution The great change that took place in France after 1789, when the people of France took over power from the King and the Church. They demanded freedom, justice, and equality for all.

Gorge A deep, narrow opening cut into hills by a river.

Gothic A style of building in the 13th and 14th centuries. Churches were tall, with high pointed arches and windows.

Heritage The culture passed down through a country's history.

Hypermarket A huge store, bigger than a supermarket, that sells a vast range of goods.

Immigrants People who have left their own country to live in another country.

Monastery A place where men belonging to a religious order, known as monks, live together.

Nationality Belonging to a particular country.

Population The number of people living in a country.

Prehistoric times The period between the first appearance of people (6 million years ago) and the invention of writing (about 3,500 years ago).

Renaissance Means rebirth in French. It is the name given to the time in the 15th and 16th century, in Europe, when new, exciting changes and discoveries happened in art and science.

Suburb An area outside a town center where people live.

3-D screens Screens that give a feeling of depth (three dimensions), rather than just a flat image.

Vineyards Fields planted with grape vines.

Index